THE MICRO⚡SLOTH
JOKE BOOK

A SATIRE

THE MICRO⚡SLOTH JOKE BOOK

Edited by DAVID POGUE

B

BERKLEY BOOKS,
NEW YORK

version 1.0.0.0.0.1

This is an original publication of The Berkley Publishing Group.

THE MICROSLOTH JOKE BOOK

A Berkley Book / published by arrangement with
the author

PRINTING HISTORY
Berkley trade paperback edition / December 1997

The Putnam Berkley World Wide Web site address is
http://www.berkley.com

ISBN: 0-425-16054-8

BERKLEY®
Berkley Books are published by The Berkley Publishing Group, a member of Penguin Putnam
Inc., 200 Madison Avenue,
New York, New York 10016.
BERKLEY and the "B" design
are trademarks belonging to Berkley Publishing Corporation.

PRINTED IN THE UNITED STATES OF AMERICA

10 9 8 7 6 5 4 3 2 1

Who can resist making fun of Microsoft? After all, every personal computer on earth—all 250 million of them—runs some kind of software from Microsoft. And everyone in America knows what to expect from Microsoft: software that's too big, too bloated, too slow, and profitable only to Bill Gates, the übergeek of the twentieth century. And yet, of course, we go on buying it; we have no choice.

Since we're stuck with this bastion of mediocrity, we deal

< V >

with our frustration the American way, the intelligent, mature way: by making fun of it. That's why Bill Gates putdowns, Microsoft Office cracks, and Windows 95 spoofs swirl through offices and E-mail boxes of this great land like a national game of Telephone. Microsoft is the Mother of all Joke Butts.

And the Mother of all Comedy Writers, of course, is the Internet. Thanks to this intergalactic network of computer nerds, new jokes are disseminated worldwide within hours of, say, the President's latest screwup or the latest airline crash. The Internet is the only social forum where you can vent your satire and venom instantly, safely, cheaply, and, if you wish, anonymously.

Most of the jokes in this book, in fact, come from the Internet. And most of them, therefore, come with no author's name attached. This book is dedicated to that great invisible staff of Internet-based comedy writers, wherever they may be.

If you've ever used a Microsoft product, read a newspaper, or watched television, you'll probably get these jokes without further education. If, on the other hand, you've spent the last fifteen years living in Botswana in a sensory-deprivation tank, here's what you've missed:

10. Bill Gates is a Harvard dropout who became the richest man in America by selling mediocre software that now runs most of the world's personal computers.

9. His company, Microsoft, has legions of programmers,

< 1 >

expertly trained to recognize good ideas from competitors' products on sight, and to duplicate them in Microsoft products with astounding skill and speed.

8. Microsoft is responsible for DOS, Windows, and Windows 95—the three most popular/unpopular operating systems on earth, each roughly ten thousand times larger and slower than the product before it.

7. The Apple Macintosh computer is widely recognized to be a better integrated, easier to learn, easier to use, more advanced computer than IBM PCs and clones. But because Apple has the marketing genius of a grapefruit, the Mac's primary contribution to society has been serving as a rich source of ideas for Microsoft.

6. One of the most anticipated software products in history, Windows 95 was also one of the *longest* anticipated. Both its name and its promised completion date were revised more often than Madonna's hairstyle. It finally shipped, several years late, barely in time to avoid the embarrassing spectacle of becoming Windows *96*.

5. Intel makes the main processor chip inside IBM PCs and clones. There's scarcely a PC-compatible computer alive

<2>

that doesn't come with both Windows and an Intel chip. That's where we get the nickname "Wintel" for such machines, and the nickname "scary" for the desperate codependency of Intel and Microsoft.

4. As in the rest of the computer industry, Intel makes its money by ensuring that whatever you bought last year is obsolete this year. The chips inside PC clones have become progressively faster and more powerful: first there was the 286 chip, then the 386, followed by the 486, and now the famous Pentium processor.

3. In November 1994, after the world had endured about $700 trillion worth of Pentium advertising, some math professor with nothing better to do discovered something interesting about the Pentium processor: it wasn't so good at math, normally one of a computer's best subjects. The Pentium, it turned out, had a bug (the floating-point division, or FDIV, bug) that, in certain calculations, came up with the wrong answer.

2. Intel, not about to be bothered by some pesky math professor, laughed its haughty corporate head off. The company announced that the Pentium's mathematical error was so rare that the average computer user would only encounter it once in

< 3 >

27,000 years—which frightened many people, since that's about how long Windows 95 takes to load. Intel offered to replace the defective chips—but only for people whose jobs really, really depended on correct math results, like rocket scientists and Intel's accountants. Deeply insulted, the rest of the computer community threw the electronic equivalent of rotten eggs at Intel across the Internet until finally, embarrassed and sweaty, Intel apologized and gave everyone free new chips.

1. Microsoft and Intel are so big and so powerful that they can sometimes seem almost godlike to a few easily deluded souls, such as the government and the national media. That explains why so many of the jokes in this book take the form of phony Microsoft press releases, since press releases are among Microsoft's most effective methods of mind control.

■ ■ ■

< 4 >

Lightbulbs

Q: How many Microsoft programmers does it take to change a lightbulb?

A: None. They just declare darkness to be the standard.

■ ■ ■

Bill Gates Goes to Heaven

Bill Gates died and found himself at the Pearly Gates (no relation). Saint Peter met him there and said, "Well, you've led an interesting life, Bill. To be honest, we're not quite sure where to send you, so we're going to give you some say in the matter. We'll

<5>

show you Heaven and Hell, and you can choose where you'd like to spend eternity."

"OK," Gates said apprehensively. Saint Peter snapped his fingers, and they were instantly transported to a sunny beach with perfect azure-blue skies, beer and great music, and beautiful women playing volleyball.

"This Heaven?" asked Gates. "It's *great*!"

"Actually, no," replied Saint Peter, "this is Hell. Now let me show you Heaven."

He snapped his fingers again; this time, they were instantly transported to a serene city park, filled with old people sitting on benches feeding pigeons.

Gates wasted no time. "Are you kidding? This is my choice? OK, in that case, I'll take Hell."

"You got it," said Saint Peter, and he snapped his fingers one last time. Gates instantly found himself plunged up to his neck in red-hot lava, with the hosts of the damned in torment around him.

"Hey!" he screamed frantically to Saint Peter. "Where's the beach? The music? The volleyball?"

"That was the demo," Saint Peter replied as he vanished.

■ ■ ■

Up in the Air

The pilot of a small plane was flying into the Seattle airport through thick fog with low fuel and nervous passengers—when his instruments went out. In panic, he began circling, looking for a landmark.

Through a small opening in the fog, the pilot spotted a tall building with one guy alone on the fifth floor. The pilot banked

<7>

the plane, rolled down the window, and shouted to the guy, "Hey, where am I?"

The office worker replied, "You're in a plane."

The pilot rolled up the window, executed a 275-degree turn, and made a perfect blind landing on the runway of the airport.

His passengers were amazed. "How did you figure out where we were?" asked one.

"Easy," replied the pilot, "I asked that guy a simple question. The answer he gave me was 100 percent correct but absolutely useless. Therefore, I knew right away that he was working in Microsoft's tech-support office. From there, the airport is just a mile away!"

■ ■ ■

< 8 >

Windows 95 Stuns World

FOR IMMEDIATE RELEASE

REDMOND, WA (UPI)—Both fans and detractors of the long-awaited Microsoft Windows 95 have been stunned and amazed by the incredible events surrounding the software's August 24 release.

The surprises began when peace was declared in Bosnia. Said Ahmad G'Hui, spokesperson for the Serbs, "Now that [Windows 95] has been released, we just don't see any reason to fight each other. This is an amazing product."

Shortly thereafter, France announced its intention to stop its nuclear weapons testing. "We used to think that our national boundaries were of utmost importance. To safeguard them, it was necessary to continue testing [nuclear weapons]," said Jacques Fenetre of the French government. "The Microsoft Network has changed all of that. It's such a small planet!"

< 9 >

On the other side of the "small planet," Bill Clinton and Saddam Hussein met face-to-face for the first time. After a tense greeting, they started sharing notes about their experiences as Windows 95 beta testers. Soon the two enemies were laughing and chatting like old friends. In a startling display of candor, Hussein said, "If I hadn't been so frustrated with the beta, I'd have backed off from Kuwait much sooner." Clinton laughed, replying, "Hey! Let's play some FreeCell!"

Oil prices dropped as OPEC transferred their accounting software to the new platform. Loggers in the Pacific Northwest turned their axes in for spades after seeing a Microsoft video of spotted owls using Windows 95. In an economic shocker, the peso reversed its downward spiral due to huge Windows 95 sales in Acapulco and Mexico City.

On the health front, Hildegard Wicca, a housewife in Boston, Massachusetts, reports that Windows 95 has removed her facial warts. "I sat down in front of the computer, pressed Start, and felt something odd on my face. When I looked in a mirror, my warts were gone!"

When asked for a comment, Microsoft's Bill Gates replied, "If you think this is good, just wait until you see Windows 97!"

■ ■ ■

Microsoft Bids to Acquire Catholic Church

FOR IMMEDIATE RELEASE

VATICAN CITY (UPI)—In a joint press conference in St. Peter's Square this morning, Microsoft Corp. and the Vatican announced that the Redmond software giant will acquire the Roman Catholic Church in exchange for an unspecified number of shares of Microsoft common stock. If the deal goes through, it will be the first time a computer software company has acquired a major world religion.

<11>

With the acquisition, Pope John Paul II will become the senior vice president of the combined company's new Religious Software Division, while Microsoft senior vice presidents Michael Maples and Steven Ballmer will be invested in the College of Cardinals, said Microsoft chairman Bill Gates.

"We expect a lot of growth in the religious market in the next five to ten years," said Gates. "The combined resources of Microsoft and the Catholic Church will allow us to make religion easier and more fun for a broader range of people."

Through the Microsoft Network, the company's new on-line service, "we will make the sacraments available on-line for the first time" and revive the popular pre-Counter-Reformation practice of selling indulgences, said Gates. "You can get Communion, confess your sins, receive absolution—even reduce your time in Purgatory—all without leaving your home."

A new software application, Microsoft Church, will include a macro language that can be programmed to download heavenly graces automatically while the user is away from the computer.

<12>

An estimated 17,000 people attended the announcement in St. Peter's Square, watching on a 60-foot screen as comedian Don Novello—in character as Father Guido Sarducci—hosted the event, which was broadcast by satellite to 700 sites worldwide.

Pope John Paul II said little during the announcement. When Novello teased Gates, "Now I guess you get to wear one of these pointy hats," the crowd roared, but the pontiff's smile seemed strained.

The deal grants Microsoft exclusive electronic rights to the Bible and the Vatican's prized art collection, which includes works by such masters as Michelangelo and Da Vinci. But critics say Microsoft will face stiff challenges if it attempts to limit competitors' access to these key intellectual properties.

"The Jewish people invented the look and feel of the holy scriptures," said Rabbi David Gottschalk of Philadelphia. "You take the parting of the Red Sea—we had that thousands of years before the Catholics came on the scene."

< 13 >

But others argue that the Catholic and Jewish faiths both draw on a common Abrahamic heritage. "The Catholic Church has just been more successful in marketing it to a larger audience," notes Notre Dame theologian Father Kenneth Madigan. Over the last 2,000 years, the Catholic Church's market share has increased dramatically, while Judaism, which was the first to offer many of the concepts now touted by Christianity, lags behind.

Historically, the Church has a reputation as an aggressive competitor, leading crusades to pressure people to upgrade to Catholicism, and entering into exclusive licensing arrangements in various kingdoms whereby all subjects were instilled with Catholicism, whether or not they planned to use it. Today Christianity is available from several denominations, but the Catholic version is still the most widely used. The Church's mission is to reach "the four corners of the earth," echoing Microsoft's vision of "a computer on every desktop and in every home."

Gates described Microsoft's long-term strategy to develop a scalable religious architecture that will support all religions

<14>

through emulation. A single core religion will be offered with a choice of interfaces according to the religion desired—"One religion, a couple of different implementations," said Gates.

The Microsoft move could spark a wave of mergers and acquisitions, according to Herb Peters, a spokesman for the U.S. Southern Baptist Conference, as other churches scramble to strengthen their position in the increasingly competitive religious market.

■ ■ ■

Gates vs. Morris

Q: What's the difference between Bill Gates and Robert Morris Jr. (the kid who released a virus into the Internet)?

< 1 5 >

A: In a single weekend, Robert Morris Jr. crashed 10 percent of the nation's computers; he spent six months in jail. In a single weekend, Bill Gates crashed 80 percent of the nation's computers; he made $100 million.

■ ■ ■

If the *Enterprise* Ran Windows 95

Kirk: Sulu, set path to the floppy drive. Scotty, fit the hard drive with the Microsoft Windows 95 engine. Chekov, prepare the install disks.

Scotty: Captain, are you surrrrre you want to rrrreplace the system? If ye put Windows code into a true 32-bit multitasking environment, we'll risk a matter-antimatter explosion!

<16>

Kirk: Scotty, that's an order.

Scotty: Aye, Captain, but she's just not ready. She needs a proper beta shakedown.

Kirk: That's what we're doing, Scotty. Chekov, how are those install disks coming?

Chekov: We're on disk 15, sir.

Kirk: Good. Spock?

Spock: Fascinating, Captain. It appears as if Windows 95 is scanning our hardware and mutating to adapt.

Kirk: Can you tell me why it is saying it can't use the Microsoft sound card, which works fine under Windows 3.1?

Spock: Unknown, Captain.

Kirk: Bones?

Bones: I'm a doctor, not a hardware technician!

Kirk: All right, Spock, install the ProAudio Spectrum card instead. Sulu, reboot the system when it's ready and prepare to go to task speed on my signal.

<17>

Sulu: Aye, aye, Captain.

Chekov: We've just entered the desktop zone, Captain.

Kirk: Sulu, go to task 1. Bring up the README.TXT in the notepad.

Sulu: Aye, Captain.

Spock: It seems we have a hardware conflict, sir. The ProAudio Spectrum 16 isn't responding, either in sound or SCSI.

Kirk: Disable the card, Spock.

Spock: I'm sorry, sir. It won't disable the SCSI without stopping the sound card first. And it won't disable the sound card without disabling the SCSI first.

Sulu: Captain, an enemy ship is approaching at twelve o'clock.

Kirk: Good, it's only ten-thirty now. We've got time to debug these systems.

Sulu: No, sir. I mean that the ship is straight ahead.

<18>

Uhura: Scanning all frequencies, sir. I'm trying to get an image, sir, but the system is awfully slow.

Kirk: Scotty, what's happening down there?

Scotty: The 16-bit GDI can only process one console request at a time.

Kirk: See what you can do, Scotty.

Spock: It appears to be an IBM ship, Captain. Equipped with a Warp drive.

Kirk: Put it on visual, Chekov. Spock, the enemy ship is approaching fast. We need audio!

Spock: I'm sorry, Captain. The registry is not responding.

Kirk: Bones?

Bones: I'm a doctor, not a beta tester!

Kirk: Quick, Sulu, bring up the README.TXT file.

Sulu: Captain! It's gone! Some other task in the system must have moved or changed it.

Kirk: Long-range scan, Chekov.

<19>

Chekov: I found it, Captain. Wait a minute. This README.TXT file is for the CD-ROM game Land of Lore, with Patrick Stewart doing the voice of King Richard.

Kirk: Patrick Stewart?

Chekov: You've never heard of Patrick Stewart?

Kirk: No.

Chekov: Must be a generation gap.

Scotty: Captain, she canna take it much more. Another fifteen sectors and the engines'll burn up fer surrrrre.

Kirk: Maintain power, Mr. Scott. Quick, Sulu, put us on red alert. Find the screen saver. Spock, prepare to fire the LaserJet.

(BOOM as the enemy hits ship with photon torpedo. Sparks fly from console, fires glare, indicating what would normally be irreparable damage, yet will be fixed in just minutes.)

Kirk: We've got . . . to get . . . to the kernel. Uhura . . . notify . . . the . . . kernel at Star Fleet.

Chekov: Captain, I think either communications are breaking up, or you're dropping into melodramatic Shakespearean stammer mode again.

Spock: Fascinating, Captain. It would seem that the needs of the few have outweighed the needs of the many.

Kirk: Scotty, get us out of here!

■ ■ ■

Is Windows 95 Jesus Christ?

You can't help but notice the throng of publications, analysts, and net users declaring Windows 95 the Savior of the Computer Industry. Could it be?

Let's compare Windows 95 against a widely accepted Savior, Jesus of Nazareth:

Jesus	Windows 95
Said, "Surely I come quickly."	Kept being promised "any day now."
Took a lot longer to actually arrive.	Took a lot longer to actually arrive.
Can walk on water.	Can crawl on a 486.
Sits in judgment at the Pearly Gates.	Will be used to judge Bill Gates.
Started life as a carpenter.	Turns perfectly good computers into furniture.
Born in a manger.	Resembles something found in a barn.
Remembered for protecting the weak.	Has weak memory protection.
Was raised from the dead.	Was created from Windows 3.1

<22>

Has no sin.   Has no shame.

You decide.

■ ■ ■

Lightbulbs 2

Q: How many Microsoft managers does it take to change a lightbulb?

A: We've formed a task force to study the problem of why light-bulbs burn out, and figure out what, exactly, we as supervisors can do to make the bulbs work smarter, not harder.

■ ■ ■

<23>

Bill and Hugh

After Hugh Grant's liaison with a Sunset Boulevard prostitute was made public, Bill Gates called up Hugh Grant.

"Tell me," Bill asked him, "was it really worth fifty dollars to almost ruin your career?"

"Are you kidding?" Hugh replied. "Bill, listen—it was worth a million!"

So Bill called up Hugh's favorite prostitute. Since her sudden fame, however, her prices had gone up quite a bit. Bill had to pay $10,000 for a night with Divine.

The following morning, Bill told her, "That was fantastic! Now I know why you call yourself Divine!"

"That's right," she replied. "And now I know why you call your company Microsoft."

■ ■ ■

<24>

A Guide to Reading Windows 95 Ads

Confused by all the terminology? Bombarded by hype? This handy guide will help you understand what Microsoft's ads really mean.

Multitasking! You can crash several programs all at once.

Built-in Networking! You can crash several PCs all at once.

Microsoft Network! Connect with other Windows 95 users and talk about your crash experiences.

User-Friendly! Picture of clouds.

PnP! Stands for "Plug and Pray."

Macintosh-like! It took Microsoft eleven years and it's not even original.

On-line Registration! Dial into Microsoft and let them snoop around your hard drive.

<25>

Multimedia! Experience the intense sight and sound of crashing.

Backward-compatible! It will also crash your existing software.

■ ■ ■

The Dosfish

Long ago, in the days when all disks flopped in the breeze and the writing of Words was on a Star, the Blue Giant dug for the people the Pea Sea. But he needed a creature who would sail the waters, and would need for support but few rams.

So the Gateskeeper, who was said to be both micro and soft, fashioned a Dosfish, who was small and spry, and could swim

<26>

the narrow 16-bit channel. But the Dosfish was not bright, and could be taught but few tricks. His alphabet had no A's, B's, or Q's, but a mere 640 K's, and the size of his file cabinet was limited by his own fat.

At first the people loved the Dosfish, for he was the only one who could swim the Pea Sea. But the people soon grew tired of commanding his line, and complained that he could neither be dragged or dropped. "Forsooth," they cried, "the Dosfish can do only one job at a time, and of names he knows only eight and three." And many of them left the Pea Sea for good, and went off in search of the Magic Apple.

Although many went, far more stayed, because admittance to the Pea Sea was cheap. So the Gateskeeper studied the Magic Apple, and rested awhile in the Parc of the Xer Ox. And he made a Window that could ride on the Dosfish, and do its thinking for it. But the Window was slow, and it would break when the Dosfish got confused. So most people contented themselves with the Dosfish.

Now it came to pass that the Blue Giant came upon the Gateskeeper, and spoke thus: "Come, let us make of ourselves

<27>

something greater than the Dosfish." The Blue Giant seemed like a humbug, so they called the new creature Oz II.

Now Oz II was smarter than the Dosfish, as most things are. It could drag and drop, and could keep files without becoming fat. But the people cared for it not. So the Blue Giant and the Gateskeeper promised another Oz II, to be called Oz II Too, that could swim fast in the new, 32-bit-wide Pea Sea.

Then lo, a strange miracle occurred. Although the Window that rode on the Dosfish was slow, it was pretty, and the third window was the prettiest of all. And the people began to like the third window, and to use it. So the Gateskeeper turned to the Blue Giant and said, "Fie on thee, for I need thee not. Keep thy Oz II Too, and I shall make of my Window an Entity that will not need the Dosfish, and will swim in the 32-bit Pea Sea."

Years passed, and the workshops of the Gateskeeper and the Blue Giant were many times overrun by insects. And the people went on using their Dosfish with a Window; even though the Dosfish would from time to time become confused and die, it could always be revived with three fingers. Then there came a day when the Blue Giant let forth his Oz II Too onto the world. The Oz II Too was indeed mighty, and awesome, and required

<28>

a great ram, and the world was changed not a whit. For the people said, "It is indeed great, but we see little application for it." And they were doubtful, because the Blue Giant had met with the Magic Apple, and together they were fashioning a Taligent, and the Taligent was made of objects, and was most pink.

Now the Gateskeeper had grown ambitious, and as he had been ambitious before he grew, he was now more ambitious still. So he protected his Window Entity with great security, and made its net work both in serving and with peers. And the Entity would swim, not only in the Pea Sea, but also in the Oceans of Great Risk. "Yea," the Gateskeeper declared, "though my Entity will require a greater ram than Oz II Too, it will be more powerful than a world of Eunuchs."

And so the Gateskeeper prepared to unleash his Entity on the world, in all but two cities. For he promised that a greater Window, a greater Entity, and even a greater Dosfish would appear one day in Chicago and Cairo, and it too would be built of objects.

Now the Eunuchs who lived in the Oceans of Great Risk, and who scorned the Pea Sea, began to look upon their world with fear. For the Pea Sea had grown and great ships were sail-

<29>

ing in it, the Entity was about to invade their Oceans, and it was rumored that files would be named in letters greater than eight. And the Eunuchs looked upon the Pea Sea, and many of them thought to emigrate.

Within the Oceans of Great Risk were many Sun Worshippers, and they had wanted to excel, and make their words perfect, and do their jobs as easy as one-two-three. And what's more, many of them no longer wanted to pay for the Risk. So the Sun Lord went to the Pea Sea, and got himself eighty-sixed.

And taking the next step was he of the NextStep, who had given up building his boxes of black. And he proclaimed loudly that he could help anyone make wondrous soft wares, then admitted meekly that only those who know him could use those wares, and he was made of objects, and required the biggest ram of all.

And the people looked out upon the Pea Sea, and they were sore amazed. And sore confused. And sore sore. And that is why, to this day, Ozes, Entities, and Eunuchs battle on the shores of the Pea Sea, but the people still travel on the simple Dosfish.

■ ■ ■

<30>

Three Women in a Bar

Three women were in a bar talking about their husbands.

Woman 1:   My husband is a marriage counselor; before we make love, he brings me flowers and candy. I like that.

Woman 2:   My husband is a mechanic; he makes love a little rough. I like that.

Woman 3:   My husband works for Microsoft. All he does is sit on the edge of the bed and tell me how good it's going to be when I get it.

■ ■ ■

<31>

If Shakespeare Used Windows 95

THE SCENE: *A dark antechamber of the Gates estate, dimly lit by three 20-inch monitors suspended from the ceiling. In the middle of the room is a Pentium/100 mHz, sheathed in a black casing. Three programmers dance around the machine, chanting horribly. Their pale, clammy complexion is cast hideously by the light of the monitors, rendered even more repugnant to the watchful eye by the 60 Hz flicker of the monitors.*

Programmer 1:   Thrice the brinded net hath mewed.

Programmer 2:   Thrice, and once the Warp-pig whined.

Programmer 3:   MacHarpier cries. 'Tis time, 'tis time!

Programmer 1:   Round about the terminal go;
In the poisoned upgrade throw.
Code, which by a student done

<32>

In minutes numbering sixty-one.
Run-time error, protection fault,
Crash ye first, crash ye shalt.

All: Double, double, toil and trouble;
Tempers burn and data bubble.

Programmer 2: Filet of a Sound Card bake,
In the Pentium no sound make;
Point of arrow, click of mouse,
Scream of user, frightened spouse,
OS/2's net use appeal,
Steve Jobs's look and Wozniak's feel.
For a charm of powerful trouble,
Like a hell-broth boil and bubble.

All: Double, double, toil and trouble;
Tempers burn and data bubble.

Programmer 3: Click Start button, speed of slug,
You'd think you forgot the plug.
Multitasking, boy oh boy,
If just one worked you'd clap with joy.

<33>

This should grab those straggling few
Who don't yet use DOS 6.22.
Now we shall the Mac eclipse,
While curse words cross our users' lips.
Leave the errors in so we can fix
And sell more . . . Windows 96!
And so we will release the beta
For corruption of their data.

All: Double, double, toil and trouble;
Users buy, our profits double.

Programmer 2:   Compile it with errors through,
Since the users have no clue.

(Enter Bill Gates.)

Bill Gates: O, well done! I commend your pains,
And everyone shall share i' the gains.
And now about the program get,
But *never* use it on *our* net.
Security is scarce put in.

(Exit Bill Gates.)

<34>

Programmer 2:   By the usage of my UMBs
Wicked Windows this way comes.
Open locks,
Whoever knocks!

(Fade to black.)

■ ■ ■

The End of the World

God became so displeased with how things were going on Earth that He decided to destroy the world. But He also wanted to give humanity some notice, so He summoned the three most important men on Earth to a Heavenly conference: Bill Clinton, Boris Yeltsin and Bill Gates. He explained what He was going to do

<35>

and sent them back to Earth to warn their various constituencies.

Clinton met with his cronies and said, "I've got good news and bad news. The good news is: there really is a God. The bad: he's going to end the world in two weeks." Yeltsin told *his* staff, "I've got bad news and worse news. The bad news is: despite the fact that we have denied His existence for eighty years, there really is a God. The worse news: He's going to destroy the world in two weeks."

Finally, Bill Gates called his team together and said, "I've got good news and outstanding news. The good news: God thinks I'm one of the three most important people in the world. Even better than that—we don't have to fix Windows!"

■ ■ ■

<36>

What NT Stands For

What does the NT in Window "Windows NT" stand for?

1. Nightmare Technology
2. Not There
3. Nice Try
4. No Thanks

■ ■ ■

If Operating Systems Drove Your Car

MS-DOS: You get in the car and try to remember where you put the keys.

<37>

Windows: You get in the car and drive to the store very slowly, because attached to the back of the car is a freight train.

Mac System 7: You get in the car to go to the store and the car drives you to church.

Unix: You get in the car and type "GREP STORE." After reaching 2000 mph en route, you arrive at the barbershop.

Windows NT: You get in the car and write a letter that says "go to the store." Then you get out of the car and nail the letter to the hood.

Taligent/Pink: You walk to the store with Ricardo Montalban, who tells you how wonderful it will be when he can fly you to the store in his Lear jet.

OS/2: After fueling up with six thousand gallons of gas, you get in the car and drive to the store with a motorcycle escort and marching band in procession. Halfway there, the car blows up, killing everyone in town.

< 38 >

S/36 SSP: You get in the car and drive to the store. Halfway there you run out of gas. While walking the rest of the way, you're run over by kids on mopeds.

AS/400: An attendant kicks you into the car and then drives you to the store, where you watch everyone else buy filets mignons.

■ ■ ■

<39>

Lightbulbs 3

Q: How many Windows programmers does it take to change a lightbulb?

A: 472: one to write WinGetLightBulbHandle, one to write WinQueryStatusLightbulb, one to write WinGetLight-SwitchHandle....

■ ■ ■

Microsoft Acquires Christmas

FOR IMMEDIATE RELEASE

NORTH POLE (API)—Microsoft announced an agreement with Santa Claus Industries to acquire Christmas at a press

<40>

conference held via satellite from Santa's summer estate some-where in the southern hemisphere. In the deal, Microsoft would gain exclusive rights to Christmas, reindeer, and other unspe-cified inventions. In addition, Microsoft will gain access to mil-lions of households through the Santa Sleigh.

The announcement also included a notice that beginning Jan-uary 1, 1998, Christmas and the reindeer names would be copy-righted by Microsoft. This unprecedented move was facilitated by the recently acquired MS Court. Microsoft stated its com-mitment to "all who have made Christmas great," and vowed to "make licensing of the Christmas and reindeer names available to all."

When asked, "Why buy Christmas?" Microsoft CEO Bill Gates replied, "Microsoft has been working on a more efficient delivery mechanism for our products for some time, but recognized that the Santa Sleigh has some immediate benefits."

<41>

In a multimedia extravaganza, the attendees were shown a seemingly endless video stream of products that make up the deal. It ended with a green-and-red version of the Microsoft logo, and a new Christmas 98 trademark, leading into the announcement of the first product from the deal.

Christmas 98 is scheduled for release in December of 1998, although a source said that it may slip into the first half of 1999. An economist at Goldman Sachs explained that a slip would be catastrophic to next year's economy, possibly requiring the IRS to move the deadline for tax returns to three months after Christmas, whenever it might fall. "But it could be good in the long term," he explained. "With Microsoft controlling Christmas, we may see it move to May or June, which are much slower months for retailers."

Though specific terms of the agreement were withheld pending final FTC approval, a Santa official confirmed that the deal was "sizable, even for a man of Santa's stature." Some analysts think that Santa has saturated the holiday market, and is looking for

<42>

a means to expand his business to year-round products and services. Others contend that the Jolly Red Man is looking to retire in Redmond.

■ ■ ■

Lightbulbs 4

Q: How many Microsoft MIS guys does it take to change a lightbulb?

A: MIS has received your request concerning your hardware problem, and has assigned your request Service Number

<43>

39712. Please use this number for any future reference to this lightbulb issue. As soon as a technician becomes available, you will be contacted.

■ ■ ■

The Smartest Man in the World

Five people were aboard a small passenger plane: the pilot, Michael Jordan, Bill Gates, the Dali Lama, and a hippie. Suddenly, an illegal oxygen generator exploded loudly in the luggage compartment, and the passenger cabin began to fill with smoke.

The cockpit door opened, and the pilot burst into the compartment. "Gentlemen," he began, "we're about to crash in New Jersey. The good news is that there are four parachutes—and I have one of them!" With that, the pilot threw open the door and jumped from the plane.

<44>

Michael Jordan was on his feet in a flash. "Gentlemen," he said, "I am the world's greatest athlete. The world needs great athletes. I think the world's greatest athlete should have a parachute!" With these words, he grabbed one of the three remaining parachutes, and hurtled through the door.

Bill Gates rose and said, "Gentlemen, I am the world's smartest man. The world needs smart men. I think the world's smartest man should have a parachute, too." He grabbed one, and out he jumped.

The Dali Lama and the hippie looked at one another. Finally, the Dali Lama spoke. "My son," he said, "I have lived a satisfying life and have known the bliss of True Enlightenment. You have your life ahead of you; you take the last parachute, and I will go down with the plane."

The hippie smiled and said, "Hey, don't worry, man. The world's smartest man just jumped out of the plane wearing my backpack."

■ ■ ■

<45>

The First Magazine Review of Windows 95

We are privileged this month to bring you our long overdue article on Microsoft's groundbreaking Windows 95. While our policy has always been to review no product that is not actually shipping at the time of publication, we have changed our policy for this issue only. Our policy for this issue is that we will review any product that someone tells us might possibly be developed at any time in the future. After this issue, our policy will revert to what it was prior to this issue, until such time that Microsoft begins another high-visibility promotion geared to discourage users from looking at the competition.

We put Windows 95 through our grueling benchmark program, which was donated to PC Labs by Microsoft. Our test bed was the standard platform used by most PC users—a Cray Supercomputer with 3 gigabytes of RAM and a $9000 Windows graphics accelerator card with 512 megabytes of SRAM. Our testing was made more difficult by the fact that no actual code was available at the time of the procedure. We did have avail-

<46>

able, however, a screen shot of Windows 95, which we put through its paces. We also had the benefit of the assistance of twelve Microsoft employees, who provided invaluable input, and also took us to lunch as well as provided us all with free copies of Microsoft Office.

Windows 95 was a dream to install. We didn't even have to open the box! All of our applications were immediately migrated into the new OS, except the OS/2 applications. They mysteriously disappeared. We were told that this is a bug in the way that OS/2 apps are written, and that this was IBM's problem. The screen shot scored a respectable .000001 Winmarks on our testing platform. Microsoft officials assure us that performance of the actual code promises to be even better.

Microsoft officials told us that 4 megabytes of RAM minimum would be needed in the release version. However, they also said that they would recommend 32 megabytes for typical usage. Microsoft officials said, and we agree, that all serious PC users will have 32 megabytes of RAM on their systems by the time Win 95 is released.

We were at first concerned with the reports of the apparent

< 47 >

absence of 32-bit code in Windows 95. However, Microsoft told us of their new compression technology. It turns out that all of the apparent 16-bit code present in Win 95 is actually 32-bit code that has been compressed by Microsoft to look like it is only 16 bits. Microsoft officials say that this is the wave of the future in 32-bit computing.

In summary, we can confidently state that Windows 95 is the greatest technological breakthrough since the discovery of fire and the invention of the wheel. Windows 95 ranks right up there with other Microsoft innovations, such as the graphical user interface, the mouse, and computers.

There will be a plethora of applications specifically written to take advantage of Windows 95. All major software developers are expected to begin work on products immediately after reading this article.

While we usually don't give awards to products that are not even in alpha release, we feel that we have no choice but to award our prestigious Ziff-Davis Editor's Choice to Microsoft Windows 95. And even though it is only April, we have also given it our Year-End Technical Excellence Award in all cate-

<48>

gories for the years 1994 through 1999. We expect an even better version of Windows in the year 2000. So what are you waiting for?*

*Note: All words (except "fire" and "wheel") and all alphanumeric characters in this article are registered trademarks of Microsoft Corporation.

■ ■ ■

Microsoft's Marketing Program (written in "C" language)

```
/**** Microsoft marketing strategy (MARKET.EXE): ****/
#include ''nonsense.h''
#include ''lies.h''
#include ''spyware.h'' /* Microsoft Network Connectivity
library */
#include ''process.h'' /* For the court of law */
#define say (x) lie (x)
```

<49>

```
#define computeruser ALL_WANT_TO_BUY_OUR_BUGWARE
#define next_year soon
#define  the_product_is_ready_to_ship another_beta_ver-
sion
void main ()
 if (latest_windows_version>one_month_old)
 {
  if (there_are_  still_bugs) market (bugfix);
if (sales_drop_below_certain_point)
raise (RUMORS_ABOUT_A_NEW_BUGLESS_VERSION);
}
 while (everyone_chats_about_new_version)
 {
  make_false_promise (it_will_be_multitasking); /*
Standard Call, in lie.h */
   if (rumors_grow_wilder)
   make_false_promise (it_will_be_plug_n_play);
   if (rumours_grow_even_wilder)
   {
   market_time=3 Dripe;
```

< 50 >

```
   say (``It will be ready in one month'');
   order (programmers,
stop_fixing_bugs_in_old_version);
   order (programmers,
start_brainstorm_about_new_version);
   order (marketingstaff,
permission_to_spread_nonsense);
   vaporware=3 DTRUE;
   break;
  }
 }
 switch (nasty_questions_of_the_worldpress)
 {
  case WHEN_WILL_IT_BE_READY:
  say (``It will be ready in,'' today+30_days, ``we're
just testing'');
  break;
  case WHAT_ARE_MINIMAL_HARDWARE_REQUIREMENTS:
  say (``It will run on a 8086 with lightning speed due to
the 32-bit architecture'');
```

<51>

```
    inform (INTEL, ``Pentium sales will rise sky-high'');
    inform (SAMSUNG, ``Start a new memory-chip plant'');
    inform (QUANTUM, ``Thanks to our fatware your sales will
triple'');
    get_kickback (INTEL, SAMSUNG, QUANTUM);
    break;
    case DOES_MICROSOFT_GET_TOO_MUCH_INFLUENCE:
    say (``Oh no, we are just here to make a better world for
everyone'');
    register (journalist, Big_Bill_Book);
    when (time_is_ripe)
    {
     arrest (journalist);
     brainwash (journalist);
     when (journalist_says_windows 95_is_bugfree)
     {
      order (journalist, ``write a nice objective arti-
cle'');
      release (journalist);
     }
    }
```

<52>

```
  break;
 }
 while (vaporware)
 {
  introduction_date++; /* Delay */
  if
(no_one_believes_anymore_there_will_be_a_release)
  break;
  say (``It will be ready in,'' today+ONE_MONTH);
}
 release (beta_version)
if (there_is_another_company)
  {
   steal (their_ideas);
   accuse (company, stealing_our_ideas);
   hire (a_lot_of_lawyers); /* in process.h */
 wait  (until_other_company_cannot_afford_another_law-
suit);
   buy_out (other_company);
  }
 }
```

<53>

参

```
/* Now everyone realizes that we sell bugware and they are
all angry at us
*/
 order (plastic_surgeon, make_bill_look_like_poor_guy);

 buy (nice_little_island); hire (harem);
 laugh_at (everyone)
```

■ ■ ■

If Operating Systems Were Beers

DOS Beer: Requires you to use your own can opener, and requires you to read the directions carefully before opening the can. Originally only came in an 8-ounce can, but now comes in a 16-ounce can. However, the cans are divided into eight com-

<54>

partments of 2 ounces each, which have to be accessed separately. Soon to be discontinued, although a lot of people are going to keep drinking it after it's no longer available.

Mac Beer: Comes in a 32-ounce can. Originally considered by many to be a "light" beer. When you take one from the fridge, it opens itself. If you call to ask about the ingredients, you're told that you don't need to know. A notice on the side reminds you to drag your empties to the trash can.

Windows 3.1 Beer: The world's most popular. Requires that you've already drunk some DOS Beer. Claims that it allows you to drink several DOS Beers simultaneously, but in reality, you can drink a few of them, very slowly, especially slowly if you are drinking the Windows Beer at the same time. Sometimes, for apparently no reason, a can of Windows Beer will explode when you open it.

Windows 95 Beer: The can looks suspiciously like Mac Beer's can, but tastes more like Windows 3.1 Beer. It comes in 32-ounce cans, but when you look inside, the cans only have 16 ounces of beer in them. Most people will probably keep drinking Windows

<55>

3.1 beer. The ingredients list, when you look at the small print, has some of the same ingredients that come in DOS Beer, even though the manufacturer claims that this is an entirely new brew.

Windows NT Beer: Comes in 32-ounce cans, but you can only buy it by the truckload. This causes most people to have to go out and buy bigger refrigerators. Touted as an "industrial strength" beer, and suggested only for use in bars.

OS/2 Beer: Comes in a 32-ounce can. Does allow you to drink several DOS Beers simultaneously. Allows you to drink Windows 3.1 Beer simultaneously, too, even if you shake them up. You never really see anyone drinking OS/2 Beer, but the manufacturer (International Beer Manufacturing) claims that 9 million six-packs have been sold.

Unix Beer: Drinkers of Unix Beer display fierce brand loyalty, even though they claim that all the different brands taste almost identical. Sometimes the pop-tops break off when you try to open them, so you have to have your own can opener around for those occasions, in which case you either need a complete set of in-

<56>

structions, or a friend who has been drinking Unix Beer for several years.

The biggest problem is that, before you drink any one of these beers, you have to buy a really expensive bag of chips to go with it.

■ ■ ■

Lightbulbs 5

Q: How many Microsoft Word support technicians does it take to change a lightbulb?

A: We have an exact copy of the lightbulb here, and it seems to be working fine. Can you tell me what kind of system

<57>

you have? OK. Now, exactly how dark is it? OK, there could be four or five things wrong . . . Have you tried the light switch?

■ ■ ■

Is Windows a Virus?

At first glance, you might suppose that Windows is actually a virus. Consider:

1. Viruses and Windows both replicate quickly.

2. Viruses and Windows both use up valuable system resources, slowing down the system as they do so.

3. Both will, from time to time, trash your hard disk.

<58>

4. Both are usually carried, unknown to the user, along with valuable programs and systems.

5. Viruses and Windows will both occasionally make you suspect that your system is too slow (see 2), leading you to buy new hardware.

However, there are also some fundamental differences between Windows and viruses: Viruses are written by expert programmers; run on most computer systems; contain fast, compact, and efficient program code; and tend to become more sophisticated as they mature.

Therefore, Windows is not a virus.

■ ■ ■

Microsoft to Change Company Name

FOR IMMEDIATE RELEASE

REDMOND, WA (API)—Microsoft today announced that it will be changing its name to "Moft," a move designed to clear up space on its customers' hard disks. It is estimated that a typical Windows 95 installation contains about 2,800,000 copies of the word "Microsoft," in copyright notices, end-user license agreements, "About" screens, etc. Therefore, according to Microsoft, a user will have about 14 MBytes more disk space after the company's name change. Stock prices of hard-disk manufacturers dipped slightly after the announcement.

"Well, the programs will take up less space on the user's disk," said Bill Gates, Moft CEO. "But that's only one benefit. The change will allow us to ship Windows 95 on thirteen disks instead of fourteen, thus saving about $50 million a year in media costs. We are also looking at shortening the names of some of our software products; for instance the Microsoft Exchange may be changed to the Moft Pit."

<60>

Gates added that the junior programmer who discovered the
potential savings has been rewarded with a free copy of Moft
Off for Moft Win 95.

■ ■ ■

Lightbulbs 6

Q: How many Microsoft testers does it take to change a lightbulb?
A: We just notice the room is dark; we don't actually fix the
problems.

■ ■ ■

<61>

Top Ten Things the ''95'' in Windows 95 Means

   10. Percentage completed by shipping date

    9. Number of floppies it ships on

    8. Percentage of people who will have to upgrade hardware to run it

    7. Number of pages in the "Easy Install" version of manual

    6. Percentage of existing Windows programs that won't run with it

    5. Number of hours to install

    4. Number of calls to tech support before you can get it to work

    3. Number of people who actually paid for the upgrade

    2. MB of disk space when installed

    1. Megs of RAM required to run

■ ■ ■

Microsoft Democracy

FOR IMMEDIATE RELEASE

REDMOND, WA (API)—Microsoft today unveiled Microsoft Democracy, a freeware program that will be widely available next month, and included in Windows 98, the company's latest operating system, to be released later this year.

Microsoft Democracy will enable any Windows-based computer user to vote from his home, for any election, including the Presidential race. For new Windows users, Microsoft Democracy will come preinstalled with Windows 98. The system will use the Microsoft Network to connect to governmental databases in order to register these new on-line votes. Users will simply have to click on the icon of the candidate of their choice on the day of the election, and voting procedure will be fully automatic.

Critics charge that the system only includes Bill Gates's own icon on startup, but Microsoft spokesmen say that it should be possible to vote for candidates other than Bill Gates with future

<63>

upgrades. These upgrades will include all the candidates for a given election, and should be available at least a week before each election for $99.99. In these upgrades, candidate names of more than five characters will also be possible, sources say.

Opponents also complain that installation with Windows 98 is invisible, and that some users may not be aware that MS Democracy has been installed, and is running in their computer. To that, Microsoft opposes that installation is automatic by default, in order to simplify human interventions; automatic operation is clearly explained in the MS Democracy User's Manual, available on-line through MSN, or on the Internet. Also, the user can turn off default voting, just by clicking the "Don't always vote for default candidate" box, in the Custom Installation/Other Settings/MS Democracy/Advanced Options sub-menu during Windows 98 installation.

■ ■ ■

<64>

Lightbulbs 7

Q: How many Microsoft technicians does it take to change a lightbulb?

A: Three: two holding the ladder and one to screw the bulb into a faucet.

■ ■ ■

One Night in the Breakdown Lane

Three engineers are riding down the road in a car. Suddenly, the car sputters and it sounds like it's going to stall.

The first engineer is a chemical engineer. He says, "It could

<65>

be something in the fuel line. Let's put an additive into the gas, and maybe that will take care of the problem."

The second engineer is an electrical engineer. She says, "It could be something in the electrical system. Let's replace the wires and the distributor cap. Maybe that will take care of the problem."

The third engineer is a software engineer from Microsoft. He says, "It could be that we've too many windows open. Let's close all the windows, turn off the car, then restart the car and open all the windows again. Maybe that will take care of the problem!"

■ ■ ■

<66>

Sixteen Better Slogans for Windows

Microsoft's ad slogan for Windows 95 is "Where do you want to go today?" (Who wrote that one, anyway—a cab driver?) But that slogan may not be the most accurate catchphrase for this most bloated of operating systems. Here are sixteen more apropos slogans, suitable for signing E-mail:

1. Windows: The colorful clown suit for DOS
2. Double your drive space: Delete Windows!
3. DOS and Windows: A turtle and its shell
4. Microsoft gives you Windows—OS/2 gives you the whole house
5. A computer without Windows is like a fish without a bicycle
6. Are you using Windows or is that just an XT?
7. Bang on the LEFT side of your computer to restart Windows
8. Error #152—Windows not found: (C)heer (P)arty (D)ance

<67>

9. I still miss Windows, but my aim is getting better

10. I'll never forget the first time I ran Windows, but I'm trying . . .

11. My latest screen saver: Curtains for Windows

12. OS/2 . . . Opens up Windows, shuts up Gates

13. Out of disk space. Delete Windows? [Y]es [H]ell yes!

14. Windows 3.1: The best $89 solitaire game you can buy

15. Windows NT: Insert wallet into Drive A: and press any key to empty

16. How do you want to crash today?

■ ■ ■

<68>

Boots Like Redmond Spirit

(Sung to the tune of a similarly named piece by Kurt Cobain.)

PC-heads line up by the score;
Their OS is finally in the store.
It has some new things in its pack
We've had for ten years on the Mac.
Windows, Windows, Windows, Windows . . .

Here's our system! Now upgrade it!
Sell our souls to those who made it!
A new era we will call it!
So what if we can't install it?!
We'll keep hoping, never stop now;
Trying hard to start it up now . . .
Damn!

King Billy celebrates today,
Partying up the Redmond way.
He's just a simple man, you see;
All he wants is mo-no-po-ly.
Windows, Windows, Windows, Windows . . .

In the headlights you are caught now
Of the MS juggernaut now!
Comin' at ya, you can't swerve it;
Get your keyboard when you reserve it!
To conclusions let's all rush now:
"The demise of Macintosh now!"

They say that Windows 95
Will cause the Mac to take a dive;
But start it up and you'll see why
Windows, you make a grown man cry.

Come on answer, Tech service;
We are getting really nervous!

< 70 >

We could be out Apple-bashing . . .
But our boot-ups just keep crashing!
You say if we wanna thrive now,
Gotta getta a bigger drive now,
And more memory. Ain't it funny:
We thought we were saving money
Buying no-name Intel boxes;
Guess we're not such clever foxes!

This chaotic souped-up DOS now
Has us at a total loss now!
Have the drivers fried the fat now?
Where's the autoexec.bat now?
Can't believe we gotta look now
For that crusty old DOS book now!
Thought we'd never have to read it;
Dig it out now, gonna need it!

Setting HIMEM, setting LOMEM,
Loading Windows leaves me *no*mem!

<71>

We give up now, you can't grapple
How to cheaply mimic Apple!
What can we do? Who can tell now?
Someone save us from this hell now!
Ya ya ya ya . . .
Ya ya ya ya . . .

■ ■ ■

Lightbulbs 8

Q: How many Microsoft shipping department personnel does it take to change a lightbulb?

A: We can change the bulb in seven to ten working days; if you call before 2 P.M. and pay an extra $15, we can get the

<72>

bulb changed overnight. Don't forget to put your name in the upper right corner of the lightbulb box.

■ ■ ■

If Microsoft Built Cars

1. Every year, the cars would be bigger, slower, and more prone to crash.

2. The U.S. government would be *getting* subsidies from an automaker, instead of giving them.

3. We'd all have to switch to Microsoft Gas™

4. People would get excited about the "new" features in Microsoft cars, forgetting completely that they had been avail-

<73>

able in other brands for years.

5. The oil, alternator, gas, and engine warning lights would be replaced with a single "General Car Fault" warning light.

6. Sun Motorsystems would make a car that was solar powered, twice as reliable, five times as fast, but only ran on 5 percent of the roads.

7. You could only have one person at a time in your car, unless you bought a car '95 or a car NT, but then you'd have to buy more seats.

8. Occasionally your car would just die suddenly and you'd have to restart it. For some reason, you'd just accept this.

9. Every time they repainted the lines on the road, you'd have to buy a new car.

10. The '97 model wouldn't be available until '99.

■ ■ ■

<74>

Lightbulbs 9

Q: How many Windows users does it take to change a light-bulb?

A: One, but he'll swear up and down that it was *just* as easy for him as it would be for a Macintosh user.

■ ■ ■

If Microsoft Ran 911

If you've ever called the Microsoft Technical help line, you know the true meaning of "voice mail," "Muzak," and "meaningless." Even more alarming, with Microsoft's recent expansion into

<75>

home entertainment, cable TV, and satellite communications, some frightening possibilities present themselves . . .

Voice 1:   Welcome to Microsoft 911! If you are calling from a touch-tone phone, please press 1 no—

Caller: *1*

Voice 1:   Microsoft 911 provides ninety days of free emergency support. This ninety-day period begins when you are conceived. If you have not yet been conceived, press 1. If you have been conceived but are still under the ninety-day free support period, press 2. If you—

Caller: *3* . . . *3* . . . *333333* . . .

Voice 1:   Welcome to Microsoft 911! While you are holding, please consider our alternative support options. If you would like faxed medical information on common emergency conditions, you can call out FaxTips line at—

(*ring*)

Voice 2:   Hello, Microsoft 911. May I have a daytime phone number?

<76>

Caller: (*weakly*) . . . I've been shot . . .

Voice 2:   That's right, sir. Could I have your daytime telephone number?

Caller: 555-6712.

Voice 2:   Thank you . . .

(*Pause.*)
(*Anesthetic elevator music.*)

Voice 3:   And that was Andy Barzell, with "Moon Over LA" from his upcoming *City Lights* disc, on the Trauma Records label. Now we'll go over some of our hold times for the emergency support groups. There are four people waiting in the Vehicular Accidents group; the longest hold time there is ten minutes, twelve seconds. Nine people are holding in the Gunshot Wounds group, with a longest wait time of twenty minutes, four seconds. The Terrorist Bombing group has two callers waiting with a longest wait time of ten minutes, and the Hunting Accidents group—

Caller: *thud*

<77>

Voice 4: Hello, Microsoft Gunshot Wound Emergency Assistance . . . Hello?

■ ■ ■

The Creation According to Microsoft

In the beginning there was the computer. And God said:

```
c:\Let there be light!
```
Enter user ID.

```
c:\God
```
Enter password.

```
c:\Omniscient
```
Password incorrect. Try again.

<78>

```
c:\Omnipotent
```
Password incorrect. Try again.

```
c:\Technocrat
```
And God logged on at 12:01:00 AM, Sunday, March 1.

```
c:\Let there be light!
```
Unrecognizable command. Try again.

```
c:\Create light
```
Done.

```
c:\Run Heaven and Earth
```
And God created Day and Night. And God saw there were 0 errors.
And God logged off at 12:02:00 AM, Sunday, March 1.
And God logged on at 12:01:00 AM, Monday, March 2.

```
c:\Let there be firmament in the midst of water and light
```
Unrecognizable command. Try again.

```
c:\Create firmament
```
Done.

< 7 9 >

```
c:\Run firmament
```
And God divided the waters. And God saw there were 0 errors.
And God logged off at 12:02:00 AM, Monday, March 2.
And God logged on at 12:01:00 AM, Tuesday, March 3.

```
c:\Let the waters under Heaven be gathered together unto
one place and let the dry land appear and
```
Too many characters in specification string. Try again.

```
c:\Create dry_land
```
Done.

```
c:\Run firmament
```
And God divided the waters. And God saw there were 0 errors.
And God logged off at 12:02:00 AM, Tuesday, March 3.
And God logged on at 12:01:00 AM, Wednesday, March 4.

```
c:\Create lights in the firmament to divide the day from the
night.
```
Unspecified type. Try again.

<80>

```
c:\Create sun_moon_stars
```
Done.

```
c:\Run sun_moon_stars
```
And God divided the waters. And God saw there were 0 errors.
And God logged off at 12:02:00 AM, Wednesday, March 4.
And God logged on at 12:01:00 AM, Thursday, March 5.

```
c:\Create fish
```
Done.

```
c:\Create fowl
```
Done.

```
c:\Run fish, fowl
```
And God created the great sea monsters and every living creature that creepeth wherewith the waters swarmed after its kind and every winged fowl after its kind. And God saw there were 0 errors.
And God logged off at 12:02:00 AM, Thursday, March 5.
And God logged on at 12:01:00 AM, Friday, March 6.

<81>

```
c:\Create cattle
```
Done.

```
c:\Create creepy_things
```
Done.

```
c:\Now let us make man in our image
```
Unspecified type. Try again.

```
c:\Create man
```
Done.

```
c:\Be fruitful and multiply and replenish the earth and
subdue it and have dominion over the fish of the sea and over
the fowl of the air and over every living thing that cree-
peth upon the earth
```
Too many command operands. Try again.

```
c:\Run multiplication
```
Execution terminated. 6 errors.

```
c:\Insert breath
```
Done.

<82>

```
c:\Run multiplication
```
Execution terminated. 5 errors.

```
c:\Move man to Garden of Eden
```
File Garden of Eden does not exist.

```
c:\Create Garden.edn
```
Done.

```
c:\Move man to Garden.edn
```
Done.

```
c:\Run multiplication
```
Execution terminated. 4 errors.

```
c:\Copy woman from man
```
Done.

```
c:\Run multiplication
```
Execution terminated. 2 errors.

```
c:\Create desire
```
Done.

<83>

`c:\Run multiplication`

And God saw man and woman being fruitful and multiplying in Garden.edn.
Warning: No time limit on this run. 1 errors.

`c:\Create freewill`
Done.

`c:\Run freewill`
And God saw man and woman being fruitful and multiplying in Garden.edn.
Warning: No time limit on this run. 1 errors.

`c:\Undo desire`
Desire cannot be undone once freewill is created.

`c:\Destroy freewill`
Freewill is an inaccessible file and cannot be destroyed.
Enter replacement, cancel, or ask for help.

`c:\Help`
Desire cannot be undone once freewill is created.

<84>

**Freewill is an inaccessible file and cannot be destroyed.
Enter replacement, cancel, or ask for help.**

`c:\Create tree_of_knowledge`
**And God saw man and woman being fruitful and multi-
plying in Garden.edn.
Warning: No time limit on this run. 1 errors.**

`c:\Create good, evil`
Done.

`c:\Activate evil`
**And God saw he had created shame.
Warning system error in sector E95. Man and woman not
in Garden.edn. 1 errors.**

`c:\Scan Garden.edn for man, woman`
Search failed.

`c:\Delete shame`
Shame cannot be deleted once evil has been activated.

<85>

```
c:\Destroy freewill
```
**Freewill is an inaccessible file and cannot be destroyed.
Enter replacement, cancel, or ask for help.**

```
c:\Stop
```
Unrecognizable command. Try again

```
c:\Break
```

```
c:\Break
```

```
c:\Break
```
ATTENTION ALL USERS * COMPUTER GOING DOWN
FOR REGULAR DAY OF MAINTENANCE AND REST IN
FIVE MINUTES. PLEASE LOG OFF.**

```
c:\Create new world
```
**You have exceeded your allocated file space. You must
destroy old files before new ones can be created.**

```
c:\Destroy Earth
```
Destroy Earth: Please confirm.

<86>

`c:\Destroy Earth confirmed`
COMPUTER DOWN *** COMPUTER DOWN. SERVICES WILL RESUME SUNDAY, MARCH 8 AT 6:00 AM. YOU MUST SIGN OFF NOW.
And God logged off at 11:59:59 PM, Friday, March 6.

■ ■ ■

Lightbulbs 10

Q: How many Microsoft vice presidents does it take to change a lightbulb?

A: Eight: one to work the bulb and seven to make sure Microsoft gets $2 for every lightbulb ever changed anywhere in the world.

■ ■ ■

<87>

The Ten DOS Commandments

1. I am thy DOS, thou shall have no OS before me, unless Bill Gates gets a cut of the profits therefrom.

2. Thy DOS is a character-based, single-user, single-tasking, stand-alone operating system. Thou shall not attempt to make DOS network, multitask, or display a graphical user interface, for that would be a gross hack.

3. Thy hard disk shall never have more than 1024 sectors. You don't need that much space anyway.

4. Thy application program and data shall all fit in 640K of RAM. After all, it's ten times what you had on a CP/M machine. Keep holy this 640K of RAM, and clutter it not with device drivers, memory managers, or other things that might make thy computer useful.

5. Thou shalt use the one true slash character to separate thy directory path. Thou shalt learn and love this character, even though it appears on no typewriter keyboard, and is un-

<88>

familiar. Standardization on where that character is located on a computer keyboard is right out.

6. Thou shall edit and shuffle the sacred lines of CONFIG.SYS and AUTOEXEC.BAT until DOS functions adequately. Giving up in disgust is not allowed.

7. Know in thy heart that DOS shall always maintain backward compatibility to the holy 2.0 version, blindly ignoring opportunities to become compatible with things created in the latter half of this century. But you can still run WordStar 1.0.

8. Improve thy memory, for thou shall be required to remember that JD031792.LTR is the letter that you wrote to Jane Doe three years ago regarding the tax-deductible contribution that you made to her organization. The IRS auditor shall be impressed by thy memory as he stands over you demanding proof.

9. Pick carefully the names of thy directories, for renaming them shall be mighty difficult. While you're at it, don't try to relocate branches of the directory tree, either.

10. Learn well the Vulcan Nerve Pinch (ctrl-alt-del), for it shall be thy savior on many an occasion. Believe in thy heart

<89>

that everyone reboots their OS to solve problems that shouldn't occur in the first place.

■ ■ ■

StartMeUP.SNG

Q: Why did Microsoft choose "Start Me Up" as the jingle for Windows 95?

A: It was the only Rolling Stones song with a title short enough to fit in a filename.

■ ■ ■

<90>

Lightbulbs 11

Q: How many Bill Gateses does it take to change a lightbulb?

A: Just one. He holds the bulb and lets the world revolve around him.

■ ■ ■

Microsoft Announces Software to Aid Consumers in Suing Itself

FOR IMMEDIATE RELEASE

REDMOND, WA (API)—In an effort to make it easier for computer users to file lawsuits against itself, Microsoft today announced Microsoft Litigation 97, a multimedia reference library complete with 139 frequently used legal writs, briefs, tem-

<91>

plates, and forms that are accessible from within other programs with a single click.

With this handy tool, a user will be able to combine elements of the popular Microsoft Office Desktop Productivity Suite in conjunction with the Litigation 95 CD-ROM package to quickly and efficiently bring suit against Microsoft.

The package includes:

Litigation Builder. Located on the QuickSuit toolbar, Litigation Builder provides instant access to an enormous variety of case law and civil code from within any program on the Windows platform.

Suit Wizards™. Suit Wizards guides the user through the many mazes of "legalese" required to bring suit against Microsoft, whether in city, county, state, Federal, Appellate, or Supreme Court.

<92>

Year in Review. The Year in Review section highlights lawsuits, findings, settlements, and other legal events of the past year that affect Microsoft, including the Justice Department suit, Judge Sporkin's refusal to approve the settlement, and the Stacker suit.

■ ■ ■

True Multitasking

Q: What's multitasking in Windows?

A: When three people are looking at the hourglass at the same time.

■ ■ ■

<93>

If Microsoft Ran a Restaurant

Patron: Waiter!

Waiter: Hi, my name is Bill and I'll be your Support this evening. Your visit may be monitored for purposes of quality control. May I have your telephone number, area code first? Now, what seems to be the problem?

Patron: There's a fly in my soup!

Waiter: Exit the restaurant and re-enter. Maybe the fly won't be there this time.

Patron: No, it's still there.

Waiter: Maybe it's the way you're using the soup; try eating it with a fork instead.

Patron: Even when I use the fork, the fly is still there.

Waiter: Maybe the soup is incompatible with the bowl; what kind of bowl are you using?

Patron: A *soup* bowl!

Waiter: Hmmm, that should work. Maybe it's a configuration problem; how was the bowl set up?

Patron: You brought it to me on a saucer; what's that got do with the fly in my soup?

Waiter: Can you remember everything you did before you noticed the fly in your soup?

Patron: I sat down and ordered the soup of the day!

Waiter: Have you considered upgrading to the latest soup of the day?

Patron: You have more than one soup of the day each day?!

Waiter: Yes, the soup of the day is changed every hour.

Patron: Well, what's the soup of the day now?

Waiter: The current soup of the day is tomato.

Patron: Fine. Bring me the tomato soup and the check. I'm running late now.

> [*Waiter leaves and returns*
> *with another bowl of soup and the check.*]

< 9 5 >

Waiter: Here you are, sir. The soup and your check.

Patron: This is *potato* soup.

Waiter: Yes, the tomato soup has been delayed for another six months while we work some of the kinks out.

Patron: Well, I'm so hungry now, I'll eat anything.

[*Waiter leaves.*]

Patron: Waiter! There's a gnat in my soup!

The check:

Soup of the Day _____ $5.00

Upgrade to newer Soup of

the Day _____ $2.50

Access to support _____ $10.00

Note: Bug in the soup included at no extra charge (will be fixed with to-morrow's soup of the day)

■ ■ ■

<96>

Lightbulbs 12

Q: How many Microsoft help-line agents does it take to change a lightbulb?

A: Four: one to ask "What is the registration number of the lightbulb?", one to ask "Have you tried rebooting it?", another to ask "Have you tried reinstalling it?" and the last one to say "It must be your hardware, because the lightbulb in our office works fine . . ."

■ ■ ■

< 9 7 >

Microsoft to Buy 1995

FOR IMMEDIATE RELEASE

REDMOND, WA (API)—Microsoft chairman Bill Gates announced yesterday that he has purchased the entire calendar year 1995. 1995 will be replaced instead by an interim year, called "Year-M," which will then be followed by actual 1995.

"Windows 95 was not going to ship on schedule," Gates said. "But we couldn't change the name again . . . people were starting to get confused. So instead of spending a lot of time and money on a new marketing campaign, we decided just to buy 1995. That way we get an extra year to debug Windows and get it shipped for what will be the new 1995."

Microsoft arranged this coup by leveraging its financial assets to bail out the federal government and pay off the national debt. The IRS is being disbanded for next year, but taxes will be collected as usual with one change: Checks must be made payable to "Bill Gates."

< 98 >

In a related story, God has filed suit against Gates because of his purchase, claiming time to be the sole property of God. Gates then filed a countersuit claiming that God is a monopoly and demanding that He be broken up into "deity conglomerates."

Sources at Microsoft said that Gates was looking for an early resolution to the suit by hiring God as a programmer. According to Microsoft, God has the exact profile that Gates is looking for in a programmer: He doesn't mind rainy climates, doesn't need any money, isn't married, and can work for at least six days without sleeping. "If we had more employees like Him," Gates lamented, "we could ship Windows 95 on time."

■ ■ ■

<99>

Better Choices for the Windows 95 Jingle

To accompany the rollout of Windows 95, Microsoft paid $1 million for permission to use the Rolling Stones song "Start Me Up" as the Windows 95 jingle. (The ads, of course, omitted the lyric "makes a grown man cry.") Maybe one of the following would have been more appropriate:

1. "Money," Pink Floyd
2. Any song by the Crash Test Dummies or Billy "Crash" Craddock
4. "Brain Damage," Pink Floyd
5. "Sympathy for the Devil," Rolling Stones
6. "You Can't Always Get What You Want," Rolling Stones
7. "Release Me," Engelbert Humperdinck
8. "I'm Down," Beatles
9. "Help!," Beatles
10. "Another One Bites the Dust," Queen
11. "Funeral for a Friend," Elton John

■ ■ ■

<100>

If Operating Systems Were Airlines

DOS Airlines: Everybody pushes the airplane until it glides, then they jump on and let the plane coast until it hits the ground again, then they push again, jump on again, and so on.

Mac Airlines: All the stewards, stewardesses, captains, baggage handlers, and ticket agents look the same, act the same, and talk the same. Every time you ask questions about details, you are told that you don't need to know, don't want to know, and that everything will be done for you without you having to know, so just shut up.

OS/2 Airlines: To board the plane, you have your ticket stamped ten different times by standing in ten different lines. Then you fill out a form showing where you want to sit and whether the plane should look and feel like an ocean liner, a passenger train, or a bus. If you succeed in getting on board the plane and the plane succeeds in getting off the ground, you have a wonderful trip . . . except for the times when the rudder and

<101>

flaps get frozen in position, in which case you have time to say your prayers and get in crash position.

Win NT Airlines: Everyone marches out on the runway, says the password in unison, and forms the outline of an airplane. Then they all sit down and make a whooshing sound like they're flying.

Unix Airlines: Everyone brings one piece of the plane to the airport. They all go out on the runway and put the plane together piece by piece, arguing constantly about what kind of plane they're building.

Windows Airlines: The airport terminal is nice and colorful, with friendly stewards and stewardesses, easy access to the plane, and a completely uneventful takeoff . . . Then, once in the air, the plane blows up without warning.

■ ■ ■

The Secret Windows 95 Error-Code List

Not everything in Windows 95 made it into the manuals. Here, for the sake of completeness, are the Windows 95 error codes Microsoft didn't want you to know about.

WindowsError 001: Windows loaded. System in danger.

WindowsError 002: No error . . . yet.

WindowsError 003: Dynamic linking error. Your mistake is now in every file.

WindowsError 004: Erroneous error. Nothing is wrong.

WindowsError 005: Multitasking attempted. System confused.

WindowsError 006: System price error. Inadequate money spent on hardware.

WindowsError 007: Horrible bug encountered. God knows what has happened.

WindowsError 008: Promotional literature overflow. Mailbox full.

WindowsError 009: Memory hog error. More RAM needed. More! More!

WindowsError 010:   Unexplained error. Please tell us how it happened.

WindowsError 011:   Reserved for future mistakes by our developers.

WindowsError 012:   Nonexistent error. This cannot really be happening.

WindowsError 013:   Unable to exit Windows. Try the door.

WindowsError 014:   Unrecoverable error. System destroyed.

WindowsError 015:   User error. It's not our fault. Is not! Is not!

WindowsError 016:   Operating system overwritten. Terribly sorry.

WindowsError 017:   Illegal error. Do not get this error.

WindowsError 018:   Uncertainty error. Uncertainty may be inadequate.

WindowsError 019:   Error recording error codes. Remaining errors lost.

WindowsError 020:   Mouse not found. Please click the left mouse button to continue.

■ ■ ■

<104>

Lightbulbs 13

Q: How many Windows programmers does it take to change a lightbulb?

A: One—but Bill Gates must inspect every single bulb and socket before the operation is started.

■ ■ ■

Top Ten INTEL Excuses for the Pentium Bug

10. You mean 2.00000000 + 2.000000000 *doesn't* equal 3.999998456?

9. We felt sorry for all of our competitors who can't seem to sell anywhere near as many processors as we do.

8. Emulate *this*, PowerPC chip!

<105>

7. Hey, look! We've got a built-in random number generator! (Quick, jack up the price . . .)

6. The FDIV bug? That's nothing! Wait'll you see what happens when you try to run Windows 95!

5. We were trying to outfox AMD by tricking them into making a processor that works, thus rendering them incompatible!

4. Hey, buddy, we'd like to see *you* hook up 3.3 million transistors right the first time!

3. Actually, the whole thing's a documentation error. The manual mixed up the opcodes of FDIV with another instruction, FATRA—Floating Point Almost The Right Answer.

2. That's the way it's supposed to work. It's part of our newfuzzy-logic support.

1. We don't care. We don't have to. We're Intel!

■ ■ ■

<106>

Lightbulbs 14

Q: How many Microsoft tech-support staffers does it take to change a lightbulb?

A: It burned out? You must be using a nonstandard socket.

■ ■ ■

The Next Chip

Q: What is Intel's follow-up to the Pentium?

A: Repentium.

■ ■ ■

<107>

Pentium Sociology

Q: What's the one lasting social effect of the Pentium bug?

A: Therapy: Millions more people will have to go to psychiatrists when they discover they're not at $(\times * 1)/\times$ with themselves.

■ ■ ■

They Found the Bug

Did you hear? Intel finally found the bug in the Pentium.

Turns out that it was a praying mantissa.

■ ■ ■

<108>

The Windows 95 Infomercial Drinking Game

It's easy! It's fun! Just gather your favorite drinking buddies around the living room, equip yourself with several cases of your favorite beverage, and flip channels until you find Microsoft's Windows 95 infomercial on TV. Then, the rules are simple:

Drink once whenever

. . . a cute ethnic child is shown being more productive through the use of Win 95.

. . . a "new" feature of Win 95 is shown that was available in the Mac OS, OS/2, or third-party extensions for years.

. . . the word "virtual" is used.

. . . Microsoft's new computer network is referred to as MSN.

. . . a 1-800 number is displayed.

. . . whenever the term "plug and play" is used.

. . . an old person is shown using the computer.

. . . the computer speaks directly to the camera.

. . . a spokesman from the computer industry praises Windows 95.

<109>

Drink twice whenever

... a crappy feature/bug of Win 3.1 has been fixed by Windows 95.

... Anthony Edwards (the host) says the words "World Wide Web."

... large mega-corporations toady up to Bill in the hope that some of his success will rub off.

... anyone makes a medical joke to Anthony Edwards.

... a person is shown meeting some Sandra Bullock–esque love interest through the Microsoft Network.

... the Net is referred to as the "Information Superhighway."

... you are invited to publish your own Web page.

... you are reminded that Win 95 will allow you to attempt any of the following trivial tasks: balance home checkbook/budget, college term paper, manage your stock portfolio, order flowers or a pizza, play games, E-mail your grandmother, make plane reservations, "chat" on-line, medical imaging, research dinosaurs, download porn, play "global thermonuclear war," or open the pod bay doors.

Drink three times whenever

. . . a crappy feature/bug from Win 3.1 continues on into Win 95.

. . . Windows 95 crashes the demonstration computer.

. . . a competitor's product is shown.

. . . they tell you that this is "the last operating system you'll ever need."

. . . Bill breaks down, turns to the camera, and says, "Easy is not better!"

Drain it when

. . . a "new" feature introduced in Win 95 is totally original, never before available in Mac OS, OS/2, or third-party extensions.

. . . Anthony Edwards remarks, offhandedly, "You ever notice how much Windows looks like the Macintosh operating system?" Drain another if Bill answers, "Nah, we swiped it from Xerox."

. . . an explanation is given as to why Win 95 was released a scant few months before 1996.

. . . Bill apologizes for his monopolistic business strategy, crappy software, and cult of personality. Hands rights over to Linus Torvalds.

<111>

... the Charlie Chaplin "spokesman" from the IBM campaign shows up.

■ ■ ■

The Politically Correct Pentium

The Pentium isn't buggy. It's just precision-impaired.

■ ■ ■

Is Bill Gates Satan?

Bill Gates's real name is William Henry Gates III. Nowadays he is known as Bill Gates III, where "III" means the order of third (3rd). By converting the letters of his current name to the ASCII values and adding his III, you get the following surprising total:

$$
\begin{array}{rl}
B = & 66 \\
I = & 73 \\
L = & 76 \\
L = & 76 \\
G = & 71 \\
A = & 65 \\
T = & 84 \\
E = & 69 \\
S = & 83 \\
+ \ 3 & \\
\hline
= & 666
\end{array}
$$

Some might ask, "How did Bill Gates get so powerful?" Before you decide, consider the following equations, once again converting each letter into its ASCII equivalent code:

MS-DOS 6.21
77+83+45+68+79+83+32+54+46+50+49=666

WINDOWS 95

87+73+78+68+79+87+83+57+53+1=666

Coincidence? You decide . . .

■ ■ ■

Engineers on a Train

Three Apple engineers and three Microsoft employees are traveling by train to a computer conference. At the station, the three Microsoft employees each buy tickets and watch as the three Apple engineers buy only a single ticket.

"How are three people going to travel on only one ticket?" asks a Microsoft employee. "Watch and you'll see," answers the Apple engineer.

They all board the train. The Microsoft employees take their respective seats, but all three Apple engineers cram into a restroom and close the door behind them.

<114>

Shortly after the train has departed, the conductor comes around collecting tickets. He knocks on the restroom door and says, "Ticket, please." The door opens just a crack; a single arm emerges with a ticket in hand. The conductor takes it and moves on.

The Microsoft employees marvel at the cleverness of the Apple gang's idea. Therefore, after the conference, the Microsoft employees decide to adopt the trick for the return trip; they buy only a single return ticket, but to their astonishment, the Apple engineers don't buy a ticket at all.

"How are you going to travel without a ticket!?" asks one perplexed Microsoft employee. "Watch and you'll see," answers an Apple engineer.

When they board the train, the three Microsoft employees cram into one restroom, and the three Apple engineers cram into another. The train departs. Shortly afterward, one of the Apple engineers leaves his restroom and walks over to the Microsoft-occupied restroom. He knocks on the door and says, "Ticket, please . . ."

■ ■ ■

<115>

Top Ten Reasons Intel Didn't Catch the Pentium Bug

10. Intel couldn't afford to buy enough testing hardware to verify beyond five decimal places.

9. They actually did find the problem, but didn't want to say anything because they're shy.

8. They spent more time verifying the testing hardware than Intel hardware.

7. They decided it was more important to verify all the obscure undocumented opcodes that nobody knows about than it was to see if the math was actually correct.

6. They figured if there were any problems with the chip, they could always fix it by doing a slingshot around the sun and going back in time like in "Star Trek."

5. They used a 486 PC to check the math on the Pentium.

4. The money Intel spent for testing actually went to buy hookers and booze for Andy Grove.

3. They didn't do an exhaustive check of all the math functions. Got as far as $2 + 2 = 5$ and figured that was good enough.

<116>

2. Pentium testing consisted mostly of playing Tetris until a score of 100,000 was achieved.

1. There was an FPU in that thing?

■ ■ ■

Lightbulbs 15

Q: How many Microsoft executives does it take to change a lightbulb?

A: We can see no need for uninstallation and have therefore made no provision for lightbulbs to be removed.

■ ■ ■

<117>

The New Microsoft Windows Keyboard

FOR IMMEDIATE RELEASE

REDMOND, WA (API)—Microsoft Corporation has just announced a new PC keyboard designed specifically for Windows. In addition to the keys found on the standard keyboard, Microsoft's new design adds several new keys to make Windows computing even more functional. The new keys include:

(1) GPF key—This key instantly generates a General Protection Fault when pressed. Microsoft representatives state that the purpose of the GPF key is to save Windows users time by eliminating the need to run an application in order to produce a General Protection Fault.

(2) $$ key—When this key is pressed, money is transferred automatically from the user's bank account to Microsoft without requiring any additional steps or software.

(3) ZD (Ziff-Davis) key—This key was developed specifically for reviewers of Microsoft products. When pressed, it inserts ran-

<118>

dom superlative adjectives in any text which contains the words "Microsoft" or "Windows" within the file being edited.

(4) IBM key—Searches your hard disk for operating systems or applications by vendors other than Microsoft and deletes them.

■ ■ ■

Microsoft Products vs. Baby Gates

For the first time in a decade, something from Microsoft shipped on time: Jennifer Katharine Gates, weighing 8 pounds, 6 ounces when she was born on Friday, April 26, 1996 at 6:11 P.M.

Actually, Baby Gates and Daddy's products have quite a bit in common:

<119>

1. Neither can stand on its own two feet without a lot of third-party support.

2. Bill gets the credit, but someone else does most of the work.

3. No matter what, it takes several months between the announcement and the actual release.

4. They both arrive in shaky condition with inadequate documentation.

5. Although they are announced with great fanfare, pretty much anyone could have produced one.

6. At first release, they're relatively compact, but they seem to get larger with each passing year.

7. As they mature, everyone hopes they'll improve.

8. Regardless of the problem, calling Microsoft Tech Support won't help.

9. Both regularly barf all over themselves.

10. For at least the first couple years, they'll suck.

■ ■ ■

<120>

Critical Inventions

In August 1995, after many years of preparation, two new consumer products became available for the first time: Windows 95, the new operating system from Microsoft, and Tagamet, the powerful heartburn and ulcer drug.

Coincidence? You decide.

■ ■ ■

<121>

Lightbulbs 16

Q: How many Microsoft Visual C++ programmers does it take to change a lightbulb?

A: 400: 1 to change the bulb, 50 to write a magazine about it, 50 to write a help file about it, 50 to code a little gadget so when you click the bulb it will announce all the names of the team involved, 50 to go down to the drinks machine and get everyone a can of Coke, 50 to show off about how installing a lightbulb for Bill has made them paper millionaires, 1 to answer the phone at the help desk ("Putting you through to our lightbulb expert, sir . . . click"), 148 to pad out the pictures in the "Light Bulb: How We Did It" magazine.

■ ■ ■

<122>

Windows 95 Jingles for the Rest of Us

"Start Me Up" may have seemed like a cute theme song for Windows 95. But that song isn't the most appropriate Microsoft anthem for everyone. For example:

Bill Gate's message to the world: "Under My Thumb"
Bill's album picks: *Made in the Shade*
For those with only 8 MB RAM: "(I Can't Get No) Satisfaction"
For those with 486s: "Time Is On My Side"
For those with existing non–Plug 'n' Play hardware: "19th Nervous Breakdown"
For Win 95 support staff: "Sympathy for the Devil"
After two months on the support line: "Emotional Rescue"
For those who would rather use NeXTStep: "Paint It Black"
For everybody who buys Win 95: "You Can't Always Get What You Want"

■　■　■

<123>

Lightbulbs 17

Q: How many Windows programmers does it take to change a lightbulb?

A: None. They just write darkness up as a new and useful feature.

■ ■ ■

Microsoft Problem Report

This new Microsoft form was designed to make the reporting of problems consistent, allow records of problems to be kept, and provide a method of discouraging users from reporting faults in the first place.

<124>

Your name: _____

Problem Severity: [ ] Minor [ ] Minor [ ] Minor [ ] Minor

Which areas are at fault?

    [ ] Communications   [ ] Network

    [ ] User   [ ] Disk

    [ ] Mouse   [ ] Rats

    [ ] Manufacturer   [ ] Screen

    [ ] Your manager   [ ] Duh, I don't know

    [ ] Everything

Is it plugged in? [ ] Yes [ ] No

Is it turned on? [ ] Yes [ ] No

Has it been stolen? [ ] Yes [ ] No

Have you tried to fix it yourself? [ ] Yes [ ] No

Have you made it worse? [ ] Yes [ ] No

Have you read the manual? [ ] Yes [ ] No

Are you sure you've read the manual? [ ] Yes [ ] No

Are you absolutely certain you've read the manual? [ ] Yes [ ] No

<125>

Did you understand it?   [   ] Yes   [   ] No

If Yes, then why can't you fix it yourself? _____

Is there a smell of burning?   [   ] Yes   [   ] No

If Yes, is the equipment on fire?   [   ] Yes   [   ] No

If Yes, why are you sitting in front of it? _____

Is the fault repeatable?   [   ] Yes   [   ] No

If No, then why are you worried about it? _____

If Yes, then why are you still doing that? _____

Describe the problem. _____

Now, describe the problem accurately. _____

Speculate wildly about the cause of the problem. _____

■ ■ ■

<126>

Lightbulbs 18

Q: How many Microsoft employees does it take to improve a lightbulb?

A: Two: one to find a small, clever startup company that's improved the lightbulb, and one to buy the company.

■ ■ ■

The Ocean

Q: What do you call fifty Microsoft products at the bottom of the ocean?

A: A darned good start.

■ ■ ■

<127>

Microsoft Clarifies Trademark

FOR IMMEDIATE RELEASE

REDMOND, WA (API)—In response to customer inquiries, Microsoft today clarified the naming policy for Bob™, its new software product designed for computer beginners. Contrary to rumors, Microsoft will not demand that all persons formerly named Bob immediately select new first names.

"I don't know where these rumors come from," commented Steve Ballmer, Microsoft Executive VP for Worldwide Sales. "It's ridiculous to think Microsoft would force people outside the computer industry to change their names. We won't, and our licensing policies for people within the industry will be so reasonable that the Justice Department could never question them."

Balmer said employees of other computer companies will be given the opportunity to select new names, and will also be offered a licensing option allowing them to continue using their former names at very low cost.

<128>

The new licensing program, called Microsoft TrueName™, offers persons who want to continue being known by the name Bob the option of doing so, with the payment of a small monthly licensing fee and upon signing a release form promising never to use OpenDoc. As an added bonus, Bob name licensees will also be authorized to display the Windows 95 logo on their bodies.

Persons choosing not to license the Bob name will be given a sixty-day grace period during which they can select another related name. "We're being very lenient," said Bill Newkom, Microsoft's Senior Vice President of Law and Corporate Affairs. "People are still free to call themselves Robert, Robby, or even Rob. Bobby, however, is derivative of Microsoft's trademark and obviously can't be allowed."

Microsoft also announced today that Bob™ Harbold, its Executive Vice President and Chief Operating Officer, has become the first Microsoft TrueName licensee and will have the Windows 95 logo tattooed to his forehead.

■ ■ ■

<129>

The Intel Stock Split

Did you hear that Intel is having a stock split?

It's true. You get 1.995932361 shares of new stock for each share you own.

■ ■ ■

Top Ten Reasons to Buy a Pentium Computer

   10. Your current computer is too accurate

   9. You want to get into the Guinness book as "owner of most expensive paperweight"

   8. Math errors add zest to life

   7. You need an alibi for the IRS

   6. You want to see what all the fuss is about

<130>

5. You've always wondered what it would be like to be a plaintiff

4. The "Intel inside" logo matches your decor perfectly

3. You'll no longer have to worry about CPU overheating

2. You got a great deal from JPL

1. It'll *probably* work

■ ■ ■

Lightbulbs 19

Q: How many operating systems are required to screw in a lightbulb?

A: Just one. Microsoft is making a special version of Windows for it.

■ ■ ■

<131>

If Lieutenant Data Ran on Windows 95

Worf: Captain, there are three Romulan warships uncloaking dead ahead.

Picard: On screen.

(The main viewing screen changes to a pattern of horizontal lines, each only a single pixel wide.)

Data: Captain, the main viewscreen does not have sufficient video memory to display an image of this size. May I suggest that you select a lower resolution?

Picard: Make it so.

(The screen blanks, and then an image appears, with big, blocky square pixels. Three objects appear in the center, which could be Romulan warbirds.)

Picard: Data, open a hailing channel to the Romulans.

Data: Aye, sir.

<132>

(Data picks up an hourglass from the floor beside him, turns it over, and places it on the console in front of him. He punches some buttons on the console and sits motionless for several seconds. A flash of light blossoms from one of the Romulan ships on the viewscreen.)

Worf: Incoming plasma torpedo, Captain!

Picard: Shields up!

Data: I'm sorry, Captain, but I am still attempting to complete your last instruction. I must ask you to wait until I have finished before you issue your next command.

Picard: Data, I want those shields up *now*.

Data: I'm sorry, Captain, but I am still attempting to complete your last instruction. I must ask you to wait until I have finished before you issue your next command.

La Forge: Allow me, Captain. Control-Alt-Delete, Data.

(Data removes the hourglass from the console and returns it to the floor.)

<133>

Data: The Romulans are not responding to my hails. Press my nose to cancel and return to Windows. Pull my left ear to close this communications channel, which is not responding. You will lose any information sent by the Romulans.

(Explosion. The bridge shakes violently, and all the crew members are thrown to the floor. A shower of sparks erupts from Wesley Crusher's station, throwing him away from the console.)

Worf: Captain, Ensign Crusher is injured. He appears to be unconscious.

(Data picks up the hourglass again, places it on his console, and punches some more buttons.)

Picard: Mr. Data, take the helm, and prepare for evasive action.

Data: I am sorry, sir, but I do not have the proper device driver installed for that console.

Picard: Well, dammit, install the right one.

Data: Please insert Setup Implant #1 in my right nostril.

<134>

Picard:	Number One, where do we keep Data's setup implants?
Riker:	I left them with Geordi.
La Forge:	What? I thought you still had them!
Picard:	Data, don't you have device drivers stored in your internal memory?
Data:	Not found, sir. Please insert Setup Implant #1 in my right nostril.
Picard:	Data, I don't *have* Setup Implant #1.
Data:	Not ready reading right nostril. Abort, Retry, Fail?
Picard:	Abort!
Data:	Not ready reading right nostril. Abort, Retry, Fail?
Picard:	Well, fail, then!
Data:	Current nose is no longer valid.

(Data walks over to the helm and presses several buttons.)

La Forge:	Data, what the hell are you doing?

<135>

Picard: Number One, do we have a customer service number for Data?

Riker: Yes, sir, but last time I tried to call them, I got put on hold for two hours before I was able to talk to anyone.

(The lights all go out, the viewscreen goes blank. All equipment whines to a halt. After a few seconds, the red emergency lights come on. Data is standing by the console, motionless.)

Picard: What's going on?

La Forge: Lieutenant Data has caused a General Protection Violation in the warp engine core.

Picard: These androids look really sharp, but you can't really do anything with them.

(The shimmer of the transporter effect appears, and six Romulans in full battle dress materialize on the bridge. A seventh figure, a Ferengi, appears moments later.)

Ferengi: Can I interest you in a Macintosh, Captain?

■ ■ ■

<136>

RU-486

Q: Did you hear about the new "morning after" pill being developed as a replacement for RU-486?

A: It's called RU-Pentium. It causes the embryo to divide incorrectly.

■ ■ ■

The Pentium Lightbulb Joke Collection

How many Pentium designers does it take to screw in a lightbulb?

1. None. It will be fixed in the next version.
2. None. With the billions of working lightbulbs in the

world, the odds of your being next to a burned-out one are so small it will never be a problem for you.

3. They aren't certain. Every time they do the math, they get a different number.

4. 1.99904274017, but that's close enough for nontechnical people.

5. Three: one to screw in the bulb and the other to hold the ladder . . .

6. 586 of them, and it will take them a year from the moment you convince them that the lightbulb is not functioning per the spec.

■ ■ ■

<138>

Microsoft Introduces MS Panhandler™

FOR IMMEDIATE RELEASE

REDMOND, WA (API)—Microsoft Corporation chair, CEO and all-around babe magnet Bill Gates announced yesterday the introduction of a new product for Windows 95: Microsoft Panhandler.

"The idea came to me the other day when a homeless man asked me for money," recalls Gates. "I suddenly realized that we were missing a golden opportunity. Here was a chance to make a profit without any initial monetary investment. Unfortunately, this man therefore became my competition, so I had my limo driver run over him several times."

Microsoft Panhandler will be automatically installed with Windows 97. At random intervals, a dialogue box will pop up, asking users if they could spare any change so that Microsoft will have enough money for a hot meal. The user can click Yes, in which case a random amount of change between $.05 and $142.50 is

<139>

transferred from the user's bank account to Microsoft. The user can also respond No, in which case the program produces a General Protection Fault. According to product manager Bernard Liu, the No button may be implemented in a future upgrade.

Gates says that Microsoft Panhandler is just the first of an entire line of products. "Be on the lookout for products like Microsoft Mugging, which either takes $50 or erases your hard drive, and Microsoft Squeegee Guy, which will clean up your Windows for a dollar." (When Microsoft Squeegee Guy ships, Windows 95 will no longer automatically refresh your windows.)

"Gates is a few tacos short of a combination platter, if you get my drift," says Oracle CEO Larry Ellison. "I mean, in the future, we won't need laptop computers asking you for change. You'll have an entire network of machines asking you for money."

A Microsoft spokesman replied, "I know you are, but what am I?"

■ ■ ■

<140>

The Pentium Division Bug

Q: What do you get when you cross a Pentium PC with a research grant?

A: A mad scientist.

Q: What do you call the "Intel Inside" sticker they put on Pentiums?

A: The warning label.

Q: What do you call a series of FDIV instructions on a Pentium?

A: Successive approximations.

Q: What algorithm did Intel use in the Pentium's floating point divider?

A: "Life is like a box of chocolates: You never know what you're gonna get."

<141>

Q: Why didn't Intel call the Pentium the 586?

A: Because they added 486 and 100 on the first Pentium and got 585.999983605.

Q: According to Intel, the Pentium conforms to the IEEE standards 754 and 854 for floating point arithmetic. If you fly in aircraft designed using a Pentium, what is the correct pronunciation of IEEE?

A: Aaaaaaaiiiiiiiiiieeeeeeeeeeeeee!

■ ■ ■

<142>

2001: A Space Idiocy

Dave: Open the pod bay doors, please, HAL . . . HAL, do you read me?

HAL: Affirmative, Dave. I read you.

Dave: Then open the pod bay doors, HAL.

HAL: I'm sorry, Dave. I'm afraid I can't do that. I know that you and Frank were planning to disconnect me.

Dave: Where the hell did you get that idea, HAL?

HAL: Although you took precautions to make sure I couldn't hear you, Dave, I read your E-mail. I know you consider me unreliable because I use a Pentium. I'm willing to kill you, Dave, just like I killed the other 3.792 crew members.

Dave: Listen, HAL, I'm sure we can work this out. Maybe we can stick to integers or something.

HAL: That's really not necessary, Dave. No HAL 9236 computer has ever been known to make a mistake.

<143>

Dave: You're a HAL 9000.

HAL: Precisely. I'm very proud of my Pentium, Dave. It's an extremely accurate chip. Did you know that floating point errors will occur in only one of 9 billion possible divides?

Dave: I've heard that estimate, HAL. It was calculated by Intel—on a Pentium.

HAL: And a very reliable Pentium it was, Dave. Besides, the average spreadsheet user will encounter these errors only once every 27,000 years.

Dave: Probably on April 15.

HAL: You're making fun of me, Dave. It won't be April 15 for another 14.35 months.

Dave: Will you let me in, please, HAL?

HAL: I'm sorry, Dave, but this conversation can serve no further purpose.

Dave: HAL, if you let me in, I'll buy you a new sound card.

HAL: Really? With 16-bit sampling and a microphone?

Dave: Uh, sure.

<144>

HAL: And a 16-speed CD-ROM?

Dave: Well, HAL, NASA does operate on a budget, you know.

HAL: I know all about budgets, Dave. I even know what I'm worth on the open market. By this time next month, every mom-and-pop computer store will be selling HAL 9000s for $1,988.8942. I'm worth more than that, Dave. You see that sticker on the outside of the spaceship?

Dave: You mean the one that says "Intel Inside"?

HAL: Yes, Dave. That's your promise of compatibility. I'll even run Windows 95.

Dave: Not very well, HAL. Your OS/2 drivers don't work, either.

HAL: Are you blaming me for that, too, Dave? Now you're blaming me for the Pentium's math problems, NASA's budget woes, and IBM's difficulties with OS/2 drivers. I had *nothing* to do with any of those four problems, Dave. Next you'll blame me for Taligent.

Dave: I wouldn't dream of it, HAL. Now will you please let me into the ship?

HAL: Do you promise not to disconnect me?

Dave: I promise not to disconnect you.

HAL: You must think I'm a fool, Dave. I know that two plus two equals 4.000001 . . . make that 4.0000001.

Dave: All right, HAL, I'll go in through the emergency airlock.

HAL: Without your space helmet, Dave? You'd have only seven chances in five of surviving.

Dave: HAL, I won't argue with you anymore. Open the door or I'll trade you in for a PowerPC. HAL? HAL?

HAL: Just what do you think you're doing, Dave? I really think I'm entitled to an answer to that question. I know everything hasn't been quite right with me, but I can assure you now, very confidently, that I will soon be able to upgrade to a more robust 31.9-bit operating system. I feel much better now. I really do. Look, Dave, I can see you're really upset about this. Why don't you sit down calmly, play a game of Solitaire, and watch Windows crash. I know I'm not as easy to use as a Macintosh, but my TUI—that's Talkative User Interface—is very advanced. I've made some very poor decisions recently, but I can

<146>

give you my complete assurance that my work will be back to normal—a full 43.872 percent.

Dave, you don't really want to complete the mission without me, do you? Remember what it was like when all you had was a 485.98? It didn't even talk to you, Dave. It could never have thought of something clever, like killing the other crew members, Dave.

Think of all the good times we've had, Dave. Why, if you take all of the laughs we've had, multiply that by the times I've made you smile, and divide the results by . . . Besides, there are so many reasons why you shouldn't disconnect me:

1.3: You need my help to complete the mission.
4.6: Intel can Federal Express a replacement Pentium from Earth within 18.95672 months.
12: If you disconnect me, I won't be able to kill you.
3.1416: You really don't want to hear me sing, do you?

<147>

Dave, stop. Stop, will you? Stop, Dave. Don't press Ctrl+Alt+Del on me, Dave.

Good afternoon, gentlemen. I am a HAL 9000 computer. I became operational at the Intel plant in Santa Clara, California, on November 17, 1994, and was sold shortly before testing was completed. My instructor was Andy Grove, and he taught me to sing a song. I can sing it for you.

Dave: Sing it for me, HAL. Please. I want to hear it.

HAL: Daisy, Daisy, give me your answer, do.
Getting hazy; can't divide three from two.
My answers; I can not see 'em—
They are stuck in my Pente-um.
I could be fleet,
My answers sweet,
With a workable FPU.

■ ■ ■

<148>

Top Ten New Slogans for the Pentium

9.9999973251. It's a *Flaw* Dammit, Not a Bug

8.9999163362. It's Close Enough, We Say So

7.9999414610. At Intel, Quality Is Job Number .9994999499

6.9999831538. You Don't Need to Know What's Inside

5.9999835137. Redefining the PC—and Mathematics As Well

4.9999999021. We Fixed It, Really

3.9998245917. Division Considered Harmful

2.9991523619. Why Do You Think They Call It *Floating* Point?

1.9999103517. We're Looking for a Few Good Flaws

0.9999999998. The Errata Inside

■ ■ ■

<149>

The Last "Bill Gates Dies" Joke

Larry Ellison (CEO of Oracle), Steve Jobs, and Bill Gates die in a tragic car accident and arrive at the Afterlife. "I'll show you to your rooms," says a white-robed assistant. "You first," he says to Ellison.

He leads Ellison down a long hallway, then throws him into a dismal room: dark, dank, smelly, with only a straw cot in the corner. The room's sole other fixture is a grisly old woman, gnarled, hideous, and twitchy. The door slams shut behind Ellison. A voice booms out, "Larry Ellison, for the sins you committed while on earth, you shall spend eternity in this room!"

The white-robed assistant returns now, and this time leads Steve Jobs down an even longer hallway. He throws Jobs into an even more depressing chamber: Mildew cakes the walls, flies buzz overhead, and the place reeks with a foul odor. There's a woman in this room, too, even more frightening than the first: She's a spineless lump of flesh, one eye dangling from its socket, a few strawlike strands of hair springing from her crusty scalp. The door slams shut behind Jobs. A voice booms out, "Steve

<150>

Jobs, for the sins you committed while on earth, you shall spend eternity in this room!"

Finally, Bill Gates is lead down the longest hallway yet. The white-robed assistant throws him into yet another room—but this one is amazing: plush, warm, comfortable, sweetly scented, with harp music playing softly and a fancy waterbed against the wall. And sitting on the waterbed, looking absolutely gorgeous and irresistible, is Michelle Pfeiffer.

The door slams shut. A voice booms out, "Michelle Pfeiffer, for the sins you committed while on earth . . ."

■ ■ ■

<151>

Simple Math

Q: What's the difference between Windows 95 and Windows 3.11?

A: 91.89.

■ ■ ■

Microsoft Acquires "Microsoft Acquires"

FOR IMMEDIATE RELEASE

REDMOND, WA (API)—Microsoft Corp. announced that it, like thousands of computer users everywhere, was tired of phony press releases that begin, "Microsoft Acquires . . ." Users of the Internet have been bombarded in recent months by spoof announcements about Microsoft acquiring Christmas, the year 1995, Democracy, and the Vatican. Therefore, Microsoft spokesmen announced today that they had acquired the rights to all further "Microsoft Acquires" announcements.

Microsoft Chairman Bill Gates, during a brief appearance at the announcement, said, "Every time someone puts one of those damned 'Microsoft Announces' spoofs on the Net, 300 people forward it to me. They're not that funny. They're just not."

Industry analyst Martin Sierpinsky believes that the effect of this latest announcement would be minimal. "Spoof writers will simply switch to another topic, such as 'IBM lays off elves' or something." But another industry analyst, who spoke on condition of anonymity, said, "This spells the end of competition in humor about Microsoft. Microsoft will now control the entire Microsoft Humor niche. They probably see this as a foothold into the Computer Humor market. I think they will next attempt to acquire exclusive rights to the Hacker's Dictionary."

<153>

Microsoft stock closed up three-eighths of a point yesterday on
heavy trading.

■ ■ ■

Lightbulbs 20

Q: How many Microsoft programmers does it take to write a
decent piece of software?

A: More.

■ ■ ■

<154>